Hi! I'm Irene, the voice behind 'Cinnamon Spice & Everything Nice' where I use fresh, seasonal ingredients to create what I like to call modern comfort food.

I breathe life into much-loved, boring classics by giving them a new, unique twist. I can turn the most hated vegetables into something deliciously palatable.

I balance my savory recipes with irresistible desserts and believe homemade brownies are perfectly acceptable for breakfast.

I love to recreate my favorite junk food and restaurant meals at home where I can control the ingredients while ditching chemicals and preservatives.

I am convinced cheese is it's own food group, and when I see a piece of fruit, I imagine all the different desserts I can bake with it.

When I'm not in the kitchen you can find me eating at my favorite diner, shopping for kitchen stuff, drinking tea by the gallons, or snuggling with my Kitchen Cat, Moon, all while dreaming of my next meal.

Bacon-Wrapped Zucchini Meatloaf

Shredded zucchini ensures a juicy, tender meatloaf and the bacon wrapping will appeal to zucchini haters. Between you and me we can keep it a secret. Most of the bacon grease ends up at the bottom of the pan so your meatloaf won't be greasy.

1 + 1/4 pounds ground beef
1 packed cup shredded zucchini (use the large holes of a box grater)
1/3 cup diced yellow onion
1/3 cup diced, jarred roasted red peppers
2 minced cloves garlic
2 large eggs
scant 1/4 cup ketchup
1 tablespoon Worcestershire sauce
scant 1/2 cup seasoned bread crumbs
1/2 cup shredded sharp cheddar cheese
6 - 7 slices bacon

Preheat the oven to 400 degrees F. Line a 9x13 baking or roasting pan with foil and spray with vegetable oil. Add everything but the bacon to a large mixing bowl and combine well with a fork or your hands. Place the meatloaf mixture in the middle of the pan and form it into a loaf about 3 inches wide and 3 inches high. Start at one end and drape the bacon over the top. It may be longer on the sides but that's OK it will shrink as it cooks. Bake 50 minutes. If the bacon isn't crisp enough for yout liking turn the broiler on for about 2 minutes being sure to keep a close eye on it so it doesn't burn. Remove from the oven and let it sit 5 minutes. Use a large spatula or 2 spatulas - one on each end to move it to a platter.

Slice into wedges.

Kitchen Tip: When mixing anything with ground meat use a fork or your hands to keep it light and tender.

Lemon Chicken and Spinach Lasagna

Layers of ricotta and mozzarella cheese sandwiched between chewy lasagna noodles with a creamy chicken and spinach lemon sauce. Different but delicious.

Sauce:
2 tablespoons butter, plus more for greasing the pan
4 cloves minced garlic
2 tablespoons all-purpose flour
2 cups whole milk
1/2 cup grated Parmesan cheese, plus more for serving
2 cups cooked chopped chicken
3 cups fresh baby spinach
3 tablespoons lemon juice

Lasagna:
15 ounces ricotta cheese
2 + 1/2 cups fresh shredded mozzarella, divided
1 egg
1 tablespoon fresh chopped parsley
1 teaspoon lemon zest
12 ounces no-boil or fresh lasagna noodles

In a large frying pan melt the butter over medium-low heat. Add the garlic and cook until fragrant. Sprinkle in the flour and continue cooking 3 minutes, stirring often. Slowly whisk in the milk and turn the heat up to medium-high. Bring to a simmer and cook 3 minutes, stirring often. Slowly whisk in the Parmesan then stir in the chicken and spinach. Remove from heat. Allow it to cool down slightly then stir in the lemon juice. Taste and season well with salt and plenty of pepper. Preheat the oven to 400 degrees F. and set a baking sheet on the bottom rack to catch any drips. Butter an 8x8 or 9x9-inch deep-sided baking pan or casserole. In a medium bowl mix the ricotta, 3/4 cup mozzarella, the egg, parsley, zest and a couple pinches each of salt and pepper.

Cover the bottom of the pan with a thin layer of sauce. Top with a layer of noodles, breaking them to fit if needed. Drop half the ricotta mixture by the spoonful and gently spread out from edge to edge. Top with 1/3 of the remaining mozzarella. Add another layer of noodles and 1/3 of the chicken mixture, spreading it out from edge to edge again. Repeat the layers again - top with noodles, the rest of the ricotta, 1/2 of the remaining mozzarella and another layer of noodles. Top with 1/2 of the remaining chicken, another layer of noodles, the remaining chicken and the rest of the mozzarella. 10. Bake 30 - 35 minutes until bubbly all over and golden. If the top starts to brown too much tent it loosely with foil.
Let it set 5 - 10 minutes before cutting into squares. Serve with a sprinkling of Parmesan.

Tortellini Caprese Salad

A dependable classic gets a makeover!

12 ounces cheese tortellini (frozen or fresh)
olive oil, for drizzling

Dressing:
1/4 cup red wine vinegar
1 teaspoon Dijon mustard
2 cloves minced garlic
1/2 cup olive oil (preferably extra-virgin)
salt and pepper

Salad:
8 ounces mini mozzarella balls, cut in half (or cubed mozzarella)
8 ounces grape tomatoes, cut in half
3 ounces chopped prosciutto
1/2 cup torn, fresh basil leaves

Cook the tortellini according to package directions in plenty of well salted water to al dente. Drain well and place in a large bowl. Drizzle with a little olive oil and toss with a wooden spoon or rubber spatula to prevent them from sticking together.

Meanwhile make the dressing:
Whisk the vinegar and mustard together in a small bowl. Drizzle in the olive oil slowly while whisking. Stir in the garlic and a couple dashes salt and pepper. Add the mozzarella, tomatoes, prosciutto and basil to the tortellini. Pour the dressing over it and toss gently with a wooden spoon or rubber spatula. Season well with salt and pepper to taste.

Serve at room temperature or chilled.

Kitchen Tip: When mixing pasta and other fragile items use a wooden spoon or rubber spatula rather than a metal spoon. This will prevent breaking and tearing so fillings don't spill out and also keeps it looking nice.

Chicken Fajita Soup

A delicious and comforting Tex-Mex soup filled with all your favorite fajita flavors! Just like the classic, the toppings really make it so please don't skip them.

1 pound boneless chicken breasts*
olive oil
salt and pepper
1 large yellow onion, diced
1 green bell pepper, diced
1 red bell pepper, diced
4 cloves chopped garlic
1 tablespoon chili powder
1 teaspoon ground cumin
1 teaspoon smoked or sweet paprika
1/4 - 1/2 teaspoon ground cayenne pepper, optional
4 cups low-sodium chicken broth
1 can (14 ounce) black beans, rinsed well in a colander
1 + 1/2 cups corn, fresh or frozen
3/4 cup Minute rice (or 1 cup cooked rice)
1 cup shredded sharp cheddar cheese, plus more for serving
sour cream, for serving
tortilla chips, for serving

Cut the chicken into bite-sized cubes. Season well with salt and pepper. In a Dutch oven or soup pot heat a tablespoon of oil over medium heat. Add the chicken and cook on all sides. Remove to a bowl or dish. Add 2 tablespoons oil to the pan set over medium-low heat and cook the onions, peppers and garlic together, stirring often until they start to soften. Add the chicken back to the pot with 1 teaspoon salt, 1/4 teaspoon black pepper and all the spices. Toss to coat the chicken and vegetables with the spices. Stir in the chicken broth, 1 cup of water, the black beans and corn. Bring to a simmer and cook, stirring often 25 minutes. Taste and season with more salt and pepper or spices if needed. Stir in the rice and cheese. Continue cooking 5 - 10 minutes longer until the rice is hot and the cheese is melted. Serve garnished with a sprinkle of cheese, a dollop of sour cream and crushed chips or chips on the side for scooping/dipping.

*Or 3 cups rotisserie chicken cut into bite-sized pieces.

Kitchen Tip: Use bottled or filtered water for cooking. Sometimes faucet water has a funny taste and can possibly alter the flavor of your food.

Roasted Brussels Sprouts and Sweet Potatoes with Bacon

This will easily turn a Brussels sprouts hater into an eager eater! I know because it happened to me.

olive oil (preferably extra-virgin)
1 container fresh baby or regular Brussels sprouts (about 12 ounces)
2 big sweet potatoes, peeled and cubed
1/2 teaspoon dried thyme
sea or kosher salt and fresh black pepper
4 slices bacon
2 - 3 tablespoons fresh grated Parmesan cheese

Preheat the oven to 400 degrees F. Grease a large baking sheet or roasting pan generously with olive oil. Remove any tough outer leaves from the Brussels sprouts and slice them in half, unless you are using baby ones, in that case leave them whole. Pile the sprouts on the baking sheet along with the sweet potatoes and drizzle liberally with olive oil (about 2 tablespoons), sprinkle with thyme and season well with salt (about 1 teaspoon) and pepper (about ¼ teaspoon). Toss with your hands rubbing the oil into the vegetables and adding more olive oil if needed to coat them well. Spread them out in one layer on the baking sheet and bake about 25-30 minutes or until the sweet potatoes are tender and Brussels sprouts are lightly browned.

Meanwhile cook the bacon:

Lay it out in one layer on a small baking pan lined with foil and bake it right alongside the veggies about 12 minutes or until crispy. Drain on paper towels and crumble when cool enough to handle.

Once the vegetables are cooked through toss with the Parmesan and bacon.

Kitchen Tip: For less mess and perfect bacon – bake it! Line a baking pan with foil and lay the bacon down in one layer. Bake 12 – 15 minutes on 375 or 400 degrees F. Once the grease is cooled fold up the foil around it and discard. Hello clean pan.

Mom's Sausage Stuffing

Mom's traditional Thanksgiving stuffing, the one my entire family dreams about all year long and descends upon like a pack of starving wolves the moment the bowl hits the table because it's that good.

12 ounces pork breakfast sausage roll*
3/4 cup diced yellow onion
1/2 cup diced celery
coarse salt and fresh black pepper
1 (14 ounce) package herb seasoned stuffing
2 (14 ounce) cans of low-sodium chicken broth
3 tablespoons melted butter plus 1 tablespoon for the top, plus more for greasing the pan

1. Set a large frying pan over medium heat and brown the sausage, breaking it apart as it cooks into small crumbles. Once it's cooked remove to a large mixing bowl. If there's a lot of grease drain some of it off leaving about a tablespoon in the pan.

2. Add the onion and celery, season with salt and pepper and cook until tender, stirring often. Add it to the bowl with the sausage. Add the stuffing to the bowl and mix it with the sausage, onion and celery.

3. Pour the cans of chicken broth over it and mix well. Drizzle the melted butter over it and mix well. Cover the bowl with plastic and let sit 5 - 10 minutes.

4. Preheat the oven to 400 degrees F. and grease an 8x8 or 9x9-inch casserole or baking pan with deep sides.

5. Taste the stuffing and season with salt and pepper if needed. Stir well again and then spoon into the pan. Cut a tablespoon of butter into small pieces and dot the top with it.

6. Bake 25 minutes, uncovered for a crunchy top or covered with aluminum foil for a soft top.

*Look for it in the freezer section with the breakfast products.

Pepper Jack & Cream Cheese Stuffed Potatoes

Spicy pepper jack cheese perks up twice-baked potatoes!

4 medium to large russet potatoes, scrubbed clean
4 slices bacon
4 tablespoons butter
1/3 cup milk or half & half, plus more if needed
4 ounces cream cheese, softened
salt and fresh black pepper
1 + 1/2 cups shredded pepper jack cheese
2 tablespoons chopped chives or scallions, divided

1. Preheat the oven to 400 degrees F. Poke the potatoes a few times with a fork and wrap each one in aluminum foil. Bake until a fork goes into them easily about 1 hour.

2. Line a small baking pan with aluminum foil and lay down the bacon in a single layer. When the potatoes are cooked turn the heat down to 375 degrees F. and cook the bacon until crispy 8 - 14 minutes. Drain on a paper towel-lined plate. Turn the heat back up to 400 degrees F.

3. When the potatoes are cool enough to handle use a grapefruit spoon to scrape the insides out leaving a border of them around the edges without scraping them right down to the skin. Put the flesh in a large bowl.

4. Add the butter, milk, cream cheese and 3/4 teaspoon salt and 1/4 teaspoon black pepper to the bowl. Mash with a potato masher or with a hand mixer on low speed until combined. If the mixture seems too thick add more milk.

5. Crumble or chop the bacon and add half to the potatoes with 1 cup of the cheese and 1 tablespoon of the chives or scallions. Taste and season with more salt and pepper if needed.

6. Preheat the oven to 400 degrees F. Place the potatoes on a baking sheet and fill them with the potatoes. Sprinkle the remaining 1/2 cup cheese on top.

7. Bake 20 minutes. Sprinkle with the remaining bacon and chives.

String Bean, Bacon & Egg Salad

Serve these gussied-up string beans as a side or a complete meal since it's chock full of protein.

1 pound of fresh string beans, ends trimmed
1/3 cup diced red onion
3 hard-boiled eggs, chopped
6 slices cooked bacon, chopped
2 tablespoons white wine vinegar
1 teaspoon Dijon mustard
3 tablespoons olive oil (preferably extra-virgin)
1 clove minced garlic
salt and pepper

1. Bring a large saucepan of water to a boil and blanch the string beans 2 minutes. Fill a large bowl with ice water and plunge them into it.

2. Drain and pat dry with paper towels. Cut into 1 to 2-inch long (bite-size) pieces.

3. In a small bowl whisk the vinegar and mustard together. Slowly whisk in the oil. Stir in the garlic with a couple pinches salt and pepper.

4. Add all the salad ingredients to a large bowl, drizzle with the dressing, season generously with salt and pepper to taste and gently toss.

5. Serve at room temperature or chilled.

Skillet Chicken Cordon Blue Noodles

All the classic flavors of chicken cordon blue are found in this easy skillet pasta!

1 pound boneless chicken breasts, cubed or 2 heaping cups cooked, diced chicken
salt and pepper
2 tablespoons butter + a small pat
1 small onion, diced
3 cloves minced garlic
8 ounces egg noodles
2 tablespoons all-purpose flour
1 + 1/2 cups chicken broth
1 + 1/2 cups milk
1 tablespoon Dijon mustard
2 cups shredded Gruyere or other good-quality Swiss cheese
4 ounces your favorite deli ham, diced (like Virginia ham)
1 cup frozen sweet peas
1 tablespoon fresh chopped parsley

1. Season the chicken with salt and pepper. Heat 2 tablespoons butter in a large frying pan over medium heat and cook the chicken turning the pieces every 2 – 3 minutes so they brown on all sides.

2. Turn the heat down to medium-low and add the onion and garlic, sprinkle the flour over everything and cook 2-3 minutes, stirring often.

3. Meanwhile, cook the noodles to al dente in plenty of salted water according to package directions. Drain well and toss with a pat of butter to prevent sticking.

4. Slowly stir in the chicken broth and milk, adding a little at a time. Stir in the mustard, 1/2 teaspoon salt and 1/4 teaspoon black pepper. Bring to a simmer and cook 3 - 4 minutes, stirring often. Add the cheese and stir until melted.

5. Stir in the ham and peas. Let it come back up to a simmer and cook 2 more minutes, stirring often.

6. Stir in the parsley and remove the pan from the heat. Add the noodles, if they'll fit in the pan, if not, add the noodles to a large mixing bowl and pour the sauce over it.

7. Toss well and serve.

Broccoli Cheese Potato Puffs
{Makes 10 Puffs}

Cheddar cheese and broccoli florets tucked inside chubby little potato patties and baked until golden and delicious.

1 pound russet potatoes, scrubbed clean
2 tablespoons butter
salt and pepper
1 large egg, lightly beaten
1 heaping cup shredded sharp cheddar
2 cups cooked, chopped broccoli florets
1/4 cup grated Parmesan cheese
sour cream, for serving

1. Prick the potatoes a few times with a fork and microwave them all at once 8 minutes to start and then in 1 minute increments until a fork easily goes into them. Cool until you can easily handle them.

2. Preheat the oven to 400 degrees F. and lightly grease a large baking sheet or line with parchment.

3. Peel the potatoes and place them in a large bowl with the butter. Mash with a potato masher.

4. Add 1/2 teaspoon salt, 1/4 teaspoon black pepper, the egg and cheese. Combine well.

5. Stir in the broccoli with a wooden spoon.

6. Place the Parmesan in a small bowl.

7. Scoop up 1/4 cups of the potato mixture and pat into balls. Coat them with the Parmesan and place on the baking sheet. Flatten gently with the palm of your hand into chubby discs.

8. Bake 16 - 18 minutes until golden on the bottom. Serve with sour cream.

Chicken, Artichoke & Spinach Calzones

{Makes 4 Personal Size}

Pizza dough wrapped around a tasty filling of chicken, artichokes, spinach, ricotta and mozzarella cheese.

2 tablespoons olive oil
2 cloves garlic, minced
1 small yellow onion, diced
1 (14 ounce) can artichoke hearts, rinsed in a colander, patted dry and chopped
1 teaspoon Italian seasoning
coarse salt and fresh black pepper
red pepper flakes, optional
3 cups fresh baby spinach leaves
1 pound pizza dough
1 + 1/2 cups cooked chicken, cubed
1 + 1/2 cups ricotta cheese
1 cup shredded mozzarella cheese
flour, for dusting
1 egg, beaten with 1 tablespoon water
Parmesan cheese, for sprinkling on top
pizza sauce, for serving

Heat the oil in a large skillet or frying pan over medium-low heat. Add the garlic, onion, artichokes, Italian seasoning, a couple pinches each of salt, pepper and red pepper flakes, if using. Cook about ten minutes, stirring often until the vegetables are soft. Turn the heat off and pile the spinach leaves on top. Let cool. Meanwhile, divide the dough into four pieces as equal as you can make them. Roll each one out on a floured surface to about an 8-inch roundish oval. If the dough is hard to work with let it sit 5 - 10 minutes.

Preheat the oven to 400 degrees F. Line a large baking sheet with parchment paper or grease it well with olive oil. When the artichoke mixture is cool mix in the chicken, ricotta and mozzarella. Season with salt and pepper to taste. Place one of the dough rounds right on the baking sheet. Scoop up one-fourth of the chicken filling and place it on one half of the dough leaving a small border. Brush the edges all the way around with egg and then fold the dough over the filling. Pinch the ends together well or roll it up over itself and crimp with a fork.

Repeat until all the calzones are made. Brush them lightly all over with egg and make a slit in the top with a paring knife to let steam escape. Sprinkle the tops with sea salt and Parmesan. Bake 26 - 30 minutes until golden brown and bubbly through the slit in the top. Let them set 5 - 10 minutes before serving with warm sauce for dipping.

Havarti Broccoli Gratin with Bacon & Fried Onions

{makes 6 - 8 servings}

Take broccoli from boring to crave-worthy in 2 seconds flat! This one takes a little bit of work but is worth every moment of your precious time.

24 ounces broccoli florets
4 slices bacon
olive oil
1 large yellow onion, thinly sliced
1/4 teaspoon sugar
2 cloves garlic, minced
sea or kosher salt and black pepper
2 tablespoons butter, plus more for greasing the pan
1 + 1/2 cups milk
1 teaspoon Dijon mustard
1 + 1/2 cups shredded Havarti cheese, divided
1/2 cup shredded white cheddar cheese
2 tablespoons grated Parmesan cheese
1/4 teaspoon ground cayenne pepper, optional
2 chopped green onions

Steam the broccoli until fork tender but not mushy. Meanwhile, preheat the oven to 350 degrees F. Line a small baking pan with foil and lay out the bacon in one layer. Bake the bacon until crispy 12 - 16 minutes. Drain on a paper towel lined plate. Chop it up.

Heat 2 tablespoons oil in a medium saucepan over medium heat and add the onions and sugar. Cook, stirring often until the onions have brown spots on them 10 - 15 minutes. Add the garlic to the onions with a couple dashes each salt and pepper, cook 2 more minutes. Remove them to a bowl.

Turn the oven up to 400 degrees F. and butter an 8x8 baking pan or casserole dish. Melt the butter in the same pan you used to cook the onions, whisk in the flour and cook 2 - 3 minutes, stirring often. Whisk in the milk and mustard - bring to a simmer - cook 3 minutes. Turn the heat down to low and add 1 cup of the Havarti and the cheddar. Stir until melted.

Remove from heat and stir in the Parmesan plus 3/4 teaspoon salt, 1/4 teaspoon black pepper and the cayenne pepper. Spread the broccoli evenly in the baking pan, pour the cheese sauce over it, top with the onions, the remaining 1/2 cup Havarti and then the bacon. Bake 25 - 30 minutes until bubbly and browned on top. Sprinkle with green onions to serve.

Baked Spaghetti & Meatballs
{serves 6}

Spaghetti smothered in creamy tomato sauce and three cheeses with tender meatballs sitting on top like a prize. Spaghetti night will never be the same.

Meatballs:
olive oil and butter, for greasing the pans
1 pound ground beef
1 egg
1/3 cup Italian-seasoned bread crumbs
2 tablespoons grated Parmesan cheese
3 cloves garlic, minced
2 teaspoons fresh chopped parsley
sea or kosher salt and black pepper

Spaghetti:
8 ounces spaghetti
1 jar (24 ounces) of good quality tomato sauce
4 ounces cream cheese, softened
1 + 1/3 cups shredded mozzarella cheese
1 tablespoon Parmesan cheese, plus more for serving

1. Preheat the oven to 400 degrees F. Grease a baking sheet with sides with olive oil. In a large mixing bowl use a fork to combine the beef, egg, bread crumbs, Parmesan, garlic, parsley, 1/2 teaspoon salt and 1/8 teaspoon black pepper. Use a 1/4 cup ice cream scoop or measuring cup to portion out the meatballs. Roll into balls and bake an inch apart 16 minutes.

2. Meanwhile cook the spaghetti to al dente in plenty of salted water according to package directions. Drain and add back to the pan. Reserve ½ cup of the sauce and then mix the rest into the spaghetti.

3. In a small bowl microwave the cream cheese until soft 15 - 20 seconds. Mix the reserved sauce into it until creamy and smooth. Add it to the spaghetti, turn the heat on low and mix it gently into the spaghetti with a wooden spoon. Remove from heat.

4. Butter an 8x8 or 9x9-inch casserole dish. Add half the spaghetti, sprinkle with 1/2 cup mozzarella and 1/2 tablespoon Parmesan. Top with the remaining spaghetti, 1/2 cup mozzarella and 1/2 tablespoon Parmesan.

5. Slice the meatballs in half and place them on the top alternating between the cut side and the round side. Sprinkle the remaining 1/3 cup cheese over the meatballs. Bake 25 minutes. Let set 5 minutes before serving.

Garlic Bread Roll-ups

{makes 9 rolls}

These are best served fresh from the oven and can be made ahead, stored in the refrigerator or freezer and baked as needed.

5 tablespoons softened butter
1 heaping tablespoon minced garlic
1 scant tablespoon chopped fresh parsley
1 tablespoon grated Parmesan cheese
1 puff pastry sheet (9x9-inch), thawed

1. In a small bowl combine the butter with the garlic, parsley and Parmesan.

2. Sprinkle a work surface lightly with flour and gently unfold the pastry. Spread 3/4 of the butter mixture evenly from edge to edge.

3. Roll it up. Cover with saran wrap and refrigerate 20 - 30 minutes.

4. Preheat the oven to 400 degrees F. Line a large baking sheet with parchment paper or lightly grease with butter.

5. Slice the pastry into 1-inch rolls and set on the baking sheet 1 - 2 inches apart. Brush the tops with the remaining butter.

6. Bake 20 minutes until golden and puffed. Brush the tops again if you have any butter left.

7. Best served fresh and hot.

Chicken, Sweet Potato & Black Bean Chili

{makes 5 – 6 servings}

For a vegetarian version, omit the chicken and double the beans.

sea or kosher salt and fresh black pepper
1 pound boneless chicken breasts or 2 heaping cups rotisserie chicken cut in bite-sized pieces
olive oil
1 small onion, diced
1 small bell pepper, cut into small, thin strips
3 cloves garlic, minced
2 cups peeled, cubed sweet potatoes
2 cans (14 ounces) diced tomatoes with the juices
1 can (14 ounces) black beans, drained and rinsed
1 cup corn
1 tablespoon chili powder
1 teaspoon ground cumin
1/2 teaspoon red pepper flakes, optional
For Serving:
shredded sharp cheddar, pepper jack or monterey jack cheese
sour cream/guacamole
tortilla chips

1. Season the chicken with salt and pepper. Add 1 tablespoon oil to a Dutch oven or large soup pot set over medium heat and cook the chicken breasts on each side until cooked through in the center.

2. Remove to a cutting board and cool.

3. Add 2 tablespoons oil to the pot over medium heat and cook the onion and pepper (season with salt and pepper) until tender about 5 minutes. Add the garlic and cook until fragrant.

4. Add the sweet potatoes, tomatoes, black beans and corn. Season with the chili powder, cumin, red pepper flakes, about 1 teaspoon coarse salt and 1/4 teaspoon black pepper.

5. Cut the chicken into bite-sized pieces and add to the pot. Bring to a simmer and cook about 35 minutes, stirring every so often and adding more seasoning as needed until sweet potatoes are tender.

6. Serve with shredded cheese, sour cream and/or tortilla chips.

Stuffed Pork Chops
{serves 4 - 6}

Nothing spells heart-warming comfort better than my Mom's specialty, a pan of stuffed pork chops. This is more technique than precision. You can use any type of pork chop you like - boneless or bone-in - thick or thin – according to your personal preference.

6 ounces pork breakfast sausage roll (like Jones)
1/2 cup diced yellow onion
1/3 cup diced celery
coarse salt and fresh black pepper
1/2 of a (14 ounce) package cubed herb-seasoned stuffing (like Pepperidge Farm)
1 (14 ounce) can low-sodium chicken broth
1 tablespoon melted butter, plus more for greasing pan
4 - 6 pork chops (I like thin, center-cut)
3 or 4 skewers

1. Set a large skillet over medium heat and brown the sausage, breaking it apart as it cooks into small crumbles. Once it's cooked remove to a large mixing bowl. If there's a lot of grease drain some of it off leaving about a tablespoon in the pan.

2. Add the onion and celery to the pan, season with salt and pepper and cook until tender, stirring often. Add it to the bowl with the sausage. Add the cubed stuffing to the bowl and mix it with the sausage, onion and celery.

3. Pour the can of chicken broth over it and mix well. Drizzle the butter over it and mix well. Cover the bowl with plastic and let sit 5 - 10 minutes. Taste and season with salt and pepper if needed.

4. Preheat oven to 375 degrees F. and grease the bottom of a large roasting pan. Lay two of the chops on the bottom and then pack a layer of stuffing over top of each one. Stand one of the pork chops up on its flattest side and place the other one right up against. Repeat until all the chops are used. Stick the skewers through them to hold together.

5. Pack the remaining stuffing into all the nooks and crannies then pile whatever's left around the base of the chops. Cover loosely with aluminum foil.

6. Bake 45 minutes to 1 hour 15 minutes depending on the thickness of your chops and how many you're using – remove the foil after 30 minutes. Check one of the chops in the middle with a meat thermometer for doneness. Look for an internal temperature of 145 (for medium rare), 160 for medium and 170 for well done.

7. Let them rest 5 - 10 minutes before serving.

Baked Shrimp Parmesan
{serves 3 – 4}

Large shrimp smothered in spicy tomato sauce, mozzarella and Parmesan cheese. Serve with cooked pasta, rice, polenta or crusty bread and a salad.

1 pound large shrimp (26-30 count), deveined with tails off
olive oil
salt and pepper
1 + 1/2 cups good quality jarred Arriabatta sauce
1 + 1/2 - 2 cups shredded mozzarella cheese
2 tablespoons Parmesan cheese
chopped fresh parsley, for garnish

1. Preheat the oven to 400 degrees F. Pat the shrimp dry with paper towels.

2. Grease a large non-stick baking sheet with olive oil and spread them out in one layer.

3. Season them with salt and pepper. Top each shrimp with a scant tablespoon of sauce then about a tablespoon of mozzarella, going back over them if needed to use up all the cheese.

4. Sprinkle the Parmesan over them and then drizzle lightly with olive oil.

5. Bake 12 - 16 minutes and pull out one of the shrimps to test for doneness – they should be opaque and white on the inside.

6. Heat the broiler and with the oven door open broil the shrimp for 1 - 3 minutes, keeping a close eye on them, until the cheese is bubbly and browned.

7. Sprinkle them with parsley and serve.

Loaded Mashed Potato Crunch
{serves 8}

A giant baked potato pancake loaded with cheese, sour cream and bacon.

2.5 pounds russet potatoes
4 tablespoons butter
1/2 cup milk
sea salt and fresh black pepper
1 + 1/2 cups shredded sharp cheddar cheese, divided
olive oil, for greasing the pan
4 slices cooked and crumbled bacon
2 green onions, snipped with kitchen scissors
sour cream, for serving

1. Peel and cube the potatoes. Add to a large saucepan and cover with water. Bring to a boil and simmer until fork tender about 20 minutes.

2. Drain and add them back to the pan set over medium heat to cook off any excess water, stir for about 2 minutes then remove from heat.

3. Add the butter, milk, 1 teaspoon salt and 1/4 teaspoon black pepper. Mash with a potato masher. Mix in 3/4 cup cheddar cheese.

4. Preheat oven to 400 degrees F. Grease a non-stick 15 x 10-inch (or similar size) baking sheet with olive oil from edge to edge making sure to get the sides too.

5. Spoon the potatoes out onto the pan and spread them evenly from edge to edge. Sprinkle the remaining cheese over the top.

6. Bake about 45 - 50 minutes until the bottom and edges are browned and crispy. Sprinkle the bacon and onions over top.

7. Cut into squares and serve with sour cream.

Orange Twist Chicken

{serves 4}

Orange slices, garlic and a myriad of spices and herbs come together in this baked chicken breast recipe.

4 boneless chicken breasts
1/2 teaspoon sweet paprika
1/2 teaspoon dried thyme
1/2 teaspoon dried oregano
1/2 teaspoon dried parsley
1/2 teaspoon onion powder
1/4 teaspoon dried dill weed
1/8 teaspoon ground cayenne pepper (or more if you like it spicier)
1/2 teaspoon salt
1/2 teaspoon black pepper
1 tablespoon butter, melted
2 cloves minced garlic
1 large navel orange or 2 small, sliced into 1/3-inch thick slices and then cut in half

1. Preheat the oven to 400 degrees F. Grease a 9x13-inch baking or roasting pan and set the chicken so it's not touching in the pan.

2. In a small bowl stir all of the spices together including the salt and pepper.

3. Brush the tops of the chicken with the melted butter and sprinkle all over with the spices holding back about 1/2 teaspoon to sprinkle on the oranges.

4. Sprinkle the garlic over them then top with the orange slices and sprinkle with the remaining spices.

5. Bake until cooked through, 20 - 35 minutes, depending on their thickness, until the internal temperature on a meat thermometer reaches 165 - 174 degrees F.

6. Let them sit five minutes before serving. Spoon any juices in the bottom of the pan over them and garnish with scallions to serve.

Creamy Chicken Gnocchi Soup

{6 servings}

Fluffy clouds of potato gnocchi, tender bites of chicken and fresh spinach swimming in a sea of thick, rich broth. Soup that hugs you from the inside out.

3 tablespoons butter
2 tablespoons olive oil
3/4 cup onion, diced
1/2 cup carrots, diced
1/2 cup celery, diced
4 cloves garlic, minced
sea or kosher salt and fresh black pepper
1/3 cup all-purpose flour
4 cups chicken broth
1 + 1/2 cups half & half
2 cups cooked white meat chicken, shredded or cut into small bites
1 pound potato gnocchi, fresh or frozen
3 cups fresh baby spinach, stems removed
1 tablespoon chopped fresh basil
fresh grated Parmesan and/or Romano cheese, for serving
warm crusty bread, for serving

1. In a large soup pot or Dutch oven heat the butter and oil together over medium-low heat.

2. Add the onions, carrots, celery and garlic. Season with salt and pepper and cook until tender about 10 minutes, stirring often.

3. Sprinkle the flour over the vegetables and cook 3 minutes, stirring often. Stir in the chicken broth one cup at a time, followed by the half & half.

4. Stir in the cooked chicken. Bring up to a simmer and maintain for 20 minutes stirring often. Season with salt and pepper to taste.

5. Meanwhile, cook the gnocchi separately according to package directions. Add them to the soup along with the spinach. Simmer until the spinach is wilted.

6. Stir in the basil and remove from heat. Serve with grated cheese and warm crusty bread.

Guacamole Taco Crunch Burgers

{makes 4}

Superheroes of the burger world, these are spiced up with taco seasonings, cheddar cheese, guacamole and tortilla chips.

Burgers:
1 pound ground beef (I like sirloin)
1/2 cup grated onion
1 + 1/2 teaspoons chili powder
1 teaspoon dried oregano, crushed between fingertips (preferably Mexican)
1/2 teaspoon ground cumin
sea or kosher salt and fresh black pepper
4 slices sharp cheddar, American or Monterey jack cheese

Guacamole:
2 avocados
1 jalapeno pepper, diced, seeds and ribs removed
1 teaspoon fresh lemon juice
1/4 cup mayonnaise or sour cream
1/4 cup diced tomatoes
sea or kosher salt and fresh black pepper
1 tablespoon fresh cilantro or parsley, chopped

For Serving:
4 hamburger buns
white corn tortilla chips

1. In a large bowl using a fork combine the ground beef, onion, chili powder, oregano and cumin together. Form into 4 equal-sized patties. Season each side with salt and pepper.

2. Cook them however you like to your desired doneness - I use a George Foreman grill. During the last minute or two, melt the cheese over top.

3. While the burgers are cooking mash the avocado and mix with the jalapeno, lemon, mayo, tomatoes and cilantro. Season to taste with salt and pepper.

4. Serve the burgers on buns with generous dollops of guacamole and chips.

Salami and Mozzarella Chicken Roll-ups

{makes 4 servings}

Chicken cutlets stuffed with salami and mozzarella then baked in tomato sauce until hot and bubbly. Serve with pasta or rice.

butter, for greasing pan
1 jar (24 ounces) marinara sauce or 4 cups homemade
4 chicken cutlets or boneless chicken breasts
sea or kosher salt and fresh black pepper
4 ounces thinly sliced salami
1 + 1/2 cups shredded mozzarella cheese

1. Preheat oven to 375 degrees F. Butter a 9 x 13-inch casserole dish. Cover the bottom of the dish generously with sauce.

2. Pound out the chicken between saran wrap to an even 1/2-inch thickness using a meat mallet. Season lightly with salt and pepper on each side.

3. Working one at a time place one ounce of salami on each chicken breast starting from the thinnest end and stopping an inch from the opposite end. Sprinkle 2 heaping tablespoons of mozzarella over top and then roll up starting from the thinnest end. Secure with a toothpick and place in pan.

4. Spoon sauce over the top of each one and then pour any leftover sauce into bottom of the pan. Sprinkle the tops with the remaining mozzarella.

5. Bake 45 minutes until bubbly all over. Remove the toothpicks for serving.

Italian Chopped Salad
{serves 8}

A salad that eats like a meal! It's packed with deliciousness and everything is chopped small so you get a lot of different flavors in every bite.

Dressing:
1/2 cup olive oil (preferably extra-virgin}
2 tablespoons honey
3 tablespoons red or white wine vinegar
1 clove garlic, minced
1/2 teaspoon Italian seasoning
1/3 cup fresh grated Parmesan cheese
coarse salt and fresh black pepper, to taste

Salad:
1/4 cup finely diced red onion
3/4 cup chopped artichoke hearts
3/4 cup diced plum tomatoes, seeds removed
3/4 cup diced cucumber, seeds removed
3/4 cup chopped pepperoni or salami
3/4 cup diced mozzarella cheese
3/4 cup sliced or chopped black olives
1 can (14 ounces) chickpeas, drained and rinsed
1 cup cooked small pasta (I used anelletti)
8 cups finely chopped romaine hearts or romaine/iceberg mix
coarse salt and fresh black pepper
red pepper flakes, optional

1. In the bowl of a food processor pulse all the dressing ingredients together except the salt and pepper until smooth and creamy. Season to taste with salt and pepper. Refrigerate.

2. In a large mixing bowl toss all the salad ingredients together except the romaine, salt, pepper and red pepper.

3. When ready to serve toss with the romaine followed by the dressing a little at a time until everything is evenly coated.

4. Season to taste with salt and pepper and red pepper flakes, if desired.

Chubby Chicken Taquitos

{makes about 10}

The golden crunch of tortillas give way to a creamy chicken and cream cheese filling that is easy to love.

3 cups cooked shredded chicken (like rotisserie)
6 ounces cream cheese, softened
1/3 cup sour cream
1/2 cup salsa
1 + 1/2 cups shredded sharp cheddar cheese
1 + 1/2 cups chopped baby spinach, stems removed
coarse salt and fresh black pepper, to taste
10 - 11 (6-inch) flour or corn* tortillas
vegetable or canola oil, for frying
your choice for serving:
sour cream/guacamole/salsa/taco sauce/ranch dressing

1. In a large bowl mix together the chicken, cream cheese, sour cream, salsa, cheddar and spinach. Season to taste with salt and pepper.

2. Working with one tortilla at a time add 2 heaping tablespoons of the chicken mixture off center and spread out like a log. Roll up and set seam side down on a platter. Repeat until all the tortillas are filled and rolled.

3. Add enough oil to a large skillet (fitted with a splatter screen) to generously cover the bottom. Heat on medium heat.

4. Cook the tortillas in batches, turning to brown all sides. Remove to a paper towel lined plate to drain. Add more oil if needed between batches.

5. Serve with your choice of dunking sauce.

*If using corn tortillas wrap 3 or 4 at a time in a damp paper towel and microwave 20 seconds before filling. This will help them become pliable so they won't tear.

Roasted Garlic & Parmesan Potatoes

{serves 4 – 5}

Soft, succulent potatoes bathed generously in olive oil with Italian seasonings, garlic and Parmesan. They make a great side for meatloaf or roasted chicken.

butter, for greasing the pan
2 pounds russet potatoes
1/4 cup olive oil (preferably extra-virgin but it doesn't have to be), divided
1 teaspoon Italian seasoning, crushed between fingertips
4 minced cloves garlic
sea or kosher salt and black pepper
1/4 cup grated Parmesan cheese, divided
red pepper flakes, optional
fresh chopped parsley, for garnish

1. Preheat the oven to 400 degrees F. Generously butter an 8x8-inch casserole dish.

2. Peel and cut the potatoes in half lengthwise then lay each half flat and slice lengthwise into 1/2-inch wide half moons.

3. Place the potatoes in a big mixing bowl and toss with 2 tablespoons of oil.

4. Add the seasoning, garlic, 1 teaspoon salt, 1/2 teaspoon black pepper and half the Parmesan (plus a few pinches of red pepper flakes if you like) and toss until the potatoes are well coated.

5. Pour the potatoes into the casserole dish.

6. Sprinkle a tablespoon of Parmesan over them and drizzle with another tablespoon of oil.

7. Bake 30 minutes. Remove the pan from the oven and toss the potatoes. Sprinkle the remaining Parmesan on top and drizzle with the remaining oil.

8. Bake 25 - 30 more minutes. Toss well and season to taste with more salt and pepper if needed.

9. Scoop them into a serving dish and pour any remaining oil/spices at the bottom of the pan over them. Garnish with fresh parsley.

Parmesan & Black Pepper Biscuits

{makes 9}

Flaky, tender drop biscuits infused with Parmesan cheese and specks of black pepper. Serve with soup, stew or any type of comfort meal.

2 cups all-purpose flour
2 teaspoons baking powder
1/4 teaspoon fine/table salt
3/4 teaspoon black pepper
6 tablespoons cold butter, cut in small cubes
1/2 cup grated Parmesan cheese
3/4 cup ice cold buttermilk
3 tablespoons heavy cream
Topping:
2 tablespoons melted butter
1/4 teaspoon black pepper

1. Preheat the oven to 400 degrees F. Line a large baking sheet with parchment paper.

2. In a large bowl whisk together the flour, baking powder, salt and black pepper.

3. Use a pastry blender or 2 knives used scissor fashion to cut in the butter until small pea-sized crumbs form.

4. Stir in the Parmesan.

5. Add the buttermilk and heavy cream. Stir until just combined - don't overmix - it will be thick.

6. Scoop up the batter with 1/3 cup measure and pat into a round shape – they don't have to be perfect. Place on the baking sheet an inch or two apart. Repeat until all the biscuits are made.

7. Bake 20 - 22 minutes until lightly golden and puffed.

8. Make the topping: In a small bowl combine the melted butter with the black pepper and brush it over the hot biscuits. Repeat until it's all used up.

9. They're best served fresh while still warm.

Chicken, Strawberry & Feta Salad

{makes 2 salads}

Chicken, strawberries, feta cheese and walnuts over baby spinach and romaine hearts with honey dressing.

Dressing:
1/4 cup honey
2 tablespoons white wine vinegar
1 teaspoon dijon mustard
1/4 cup extra-virgin olive oil
sea or kosher salt and fresh black pepper

Salad:
2 packed cups baby spinach
2 packed cups chopped romaine hearts
1 heaping cup sliced strawberries
1 heaping cup chopped or shredded cooked chicken
1/3 cup crumbled feta cheese
1/4 cup chopped walnuts or sliced almonds

1. In a small bowl whisk the honey, vinegar and mustard together. Slowly whisk in the oil. Season to taste with salt and pepper.

2. In a large bowl toss the spinach, romaine and strawberries together with a drizzle or two of dressing.

3. Divide among 2 plates. Arrange the chicken over top and sprinkle with feta and nuts.

4. Serve with additional dressing, salt and pepper.

No-Bake Tiramisu Eclair Cake
{9 servings}

Tiramisu made in the style of an eclair cake with layers of mascarpone cream between espresso soaked graham crackers. One of the fastest, easiest, most delicious no-bake refrigerator cakes that will ever cross your lips!

Filling:
8 ounces mascarpone cheese (find it in the artisan cheese section)
1/2 cup sugar
1/4 teaspoon vanilla extract
3 cups very cold heavy whipping cream
1/8 teaspoon cream of tartar

Cake:
1 box (14.4 ounce) graham crackers
1 + ½ cups cooled espresso or very strong brewed coffee (I use decaf), divided
cocoa powder, for sprinkling on top
1/3 cup chopped or shaved chocolate, for the top

1. Line an 8x8-inch deep-sided baking or casserole pan with parchment paper or grease it lightly with butter. In a large mixing bowl on low speed beat the mascarpone, sugar and vanilla together until fluffy about 2 minutes.

2. In a stand mixer or large mixing bowl beat the whipping cream on medium speed to stiff peaks – when you lift the beater the cream should stick to it. Spoon the whipped cream into the bowl with the mascarpone and gently fold them together. Set aside 1 cup of the cream mixture for the top. Line the bottom of the prepared pan with a layer of graham crackers, breaking them to fit. Use a pastry brush to soak them with ¼ cup espresso.

3. Repeat with another layer of graham crackers and ¼ cup espresso. Spoon half the cream over them and spread evenly from edge to edge. Top with a layer of graham crackers and brush with ¼ cup espresso then repeat with a second layer of graham crackers and another ¼ cup espresso.

4. Spoon the remaining cream into the pan and spread it evenly from edge to edge. Top with another layer of graham crackers, brush with ¼ cup espresso, then repeat with a second layer of crackers and the remaining espresso. Spoon the cup of cream you set aside earlier over them and spread it out evenly from edge to edge. Dust the top with cocoa and scatter with chocolate.

5. Refrigerate at least 6 hours or overnight. If you used parchment paper you can remove the entire cake to a cutting board for easier cutting. Dip the knife in hot water and wipe clean after each cut.

6. Best eaten within 48 hours. Keep refrigerated.

Oven-Fried Corn Flake Chicken
{serves 4}

Crunchy, finger-licking chicken every bit as good as fried but without all the mess! A buttermilk herb marinade ensures juicy, tender results packed with great flavor.

Marinade:
1 + 1/2 cups buttermilk
1/2 teaspoon salt
1/4 teaspoon black pepper
1/4 teaspoon onion powder
1/4 teaspoon garlic powder
2 + 1/4 pounds bone-in chicken* or 1 + 1/2 pounds boneless chicken breasts
Breading:
2 eggs
2/3 cup crushed corn flake crumbs
2/3 cup Japanese panko crumbs
1 teaspoon sweet paprika
1/2 teaspoon chili powder
1/2 teaspoon dried parsley
1/2 teaspoon onion powder
1/2 teaspoon salt
1/4 teaspoon black pepper
1/4 teaspoon dried oregano
1/4 teaspoon garlic powder
1/4 teaspoon ground sage
1 tablespoon melted butter or vegetable spray

The night before or the morning of:
In a large bowl whisk the buttermilk with all the seasonings. Add the chicken pieces and turn to coat all over. Cover the bowl and refrigerate until an hour before you bake it – take it out so it's not ice cold when it goes into the oven.

Preheat the oven to 400 degrees F. Line a large, rimmed baking sheet with parchment. Set up a dredging station: In a wide shallow dish beat the eggs together. In a separate, wide shallow dish stir the panko, corn flakes and all the seasonings together then remove half of them to a small bowl and set aside. Working with one piece of chicken at a time remove it from the buttermilk with tongs and let the excess drain off, dunk it in egg, let the excess drip off then coat well with the crumbs pressing them on with your hands. Place the chicken skin side up on the baking sheet and repeat until all the chicken is coated. Add crumbs from the small bowl to the wide dish as needed. Discard any unused egg and crumbs.

Bake: Drizzle each piece lightly with the melted butter or spray lightly all over with non-stick vegetable spray. Bake 25 - 30 minutes for thighs, 45 - 50 minutes for bone-in breasts and legs, 25 – 30 minutes for boneless breasts and wings (all times are approximate). The internal temperature on a meat thermometer should read 165 degrees F and the juices should run clear.

*I use thighs.

Baked String Bean Fries with Lemon Dipping Sauce

{serves 4}

Get out of my way potato fries! Coming through with the best new french fries in town... meet the green bean fry.

1 - 2 teaspoons olive oil, plus more for greasing the pan
1/2 pound French green beans, ends trimmed
1 - 2 teaspoons cornstarch
2 eggs
1/2 cup grated Parmesan cheese
1/3 cup seasoned bread crumbs
1/3 cup Japanese panko crumbs
salt and pepper

Lemon Dipping Sauce:
1/2 cup mayonnaise
the zest of 1 lemon
a squeeze or two of fresh lemon juice
a few fresh thyme leaves, chopped

1. Preheat the oven to 400 degrees F. Grease a large, non-stick baking sheet with olive oil. In a large mixing bowl toss the green beans with the oil massaging it on with your hands. Sprinkle with cornstarch starting with 1 teaspoon and toss well. Add more cornstarch if needed to lightly coat them all over.

2. Beat the eggs with a tablespoon of water in a wide, shallow bowl. In a separate shallow bowl toss the Parmesan with both types of bread crumbs and a few good dashes of salt and pepper. Remove half of them and set aside, adding them back to the bowl as needed so they don't get gummy from the egg drips.

3. Working with a handful at a time dunk them into the egg (with one hand) then into the bread crumbs patting them on with your other, non-eggy hand. Place on the baking sheet close together but not touching. Repeat until all the string beans are coated.

4. Bake 12 minutes then turn them over (if you find that they are sticking or the coating is coming off skip this step) and bake 6 - 8 minutes longer or until golden brown all over and tender on the inside. Meanwhile whisk the mayonnaise, zest, lemon juice and thyme together.

5. Serve them fresh from the oven with the dipping sauce. They don't work well as leftovers/reheated - they get soggy.

Roasted Buffalo Cauliflower with Ranch Yogurt Dip

{4 servings as a side or appetizer}

Cauliflower florets smothered in a fiery homemade buffalo sauce with ranch yogurt dip to put out the blaze.

Dip:
1/3 cup Greek yogurt
1/3 cup sour cream
1 clove garlic, minced
1/2 teaspoon dried parsley
1/2 teaspoon dried chives
1/4 teaspoon dried dill
1/4 teaspoon onion powder
pinch each of salt and pepper

Hot Sauce:
1/2 cup hot sauce
4 tablespoons butter
scant 1/4 cup grated Parmesan cheese
1/8 teaspoon garlic powder
1/8 teaspoon black pepper

Cauliflower:
olive oil, for greasing the pan
1 medium head cauliflower (7 - 8 cups)
sea or kosher salt

In a medium bowl whisk all the dip ingredients together. Cover and refrigerate. Add the hot sauce and butter to a small saucepan set over medium-low heat. Stir to melt the butter and cook 2 minutes. Remove from heat and stir in the Parmesan, garlic powder and black pepper. Set aside to cool. Preheat the oven to 375 degrees F. Grease a large non-stick baking sheet generously with olive oil. Cut the head of cauliflower into florets - not too small - they will shrink as they cook. Place the cauliflower in a large bowl and pour the hot sauce over it. Mix until the cauliflower are well coated. Spread them out on the baking sheet and drizzle any sauce left in the bowl over them. Sprinkle lightly with salt. Bake 15 minutes. Remove the pan from the oven and toss the cauliflower, scraping up any sauce that is laying on the bottom of the pan. Spread them out again. Bake 15 more minutes. Take them out of the oven and toss again. A fork should easily go into them – if not continue baking another ten minutes or so until fork tender.

Serve warm or at room temperature with the dip.

Cream Cheese Chicken Enchiladas

{serves 6}

Chicken, cream cheese, cheddar and fresh spinach tucked inside tortillas, rolled up and smothered in a spicy sour cream sauce then baked until molten hot and bubbly.

Sauce:
1 cup chicken broth
1 can (11 ounce) Ro-tel diced tomatoes and green chiles
1 teaspoon chili powder
1/2 teaspoon ground cayenne pepper (optional)
salt and pepper
1 tablespoon cornstarch
1 cup sour cream

Filling:
8 ounces bar cream cheese, softened
3 cups cooked chicken, cut into bite-sized pieces
2 cups shredded extra sharp cheddar cheese, divided
2 packed cups fresh baby spinach, stack them and slice into thin strips
coarse salt and fresh black pepper, to taste
butter, for greasing the pan
10 (8-inch) flour tortillas

Toppings (your choice):
sour cream, diced fresh tomatoes, guacamole/diced avocado, lettuce, chopped fresh cilantro

Make the Sauce: Add the broth and Ro-tel to a blender and blend until fairly smooth. Pour it into a medium saucepan and add the chili powder and cayenne, if using, with a couple good dashes salt and pepper. Bring it up to a simmer. In a small bowl mix the cornstarch with 2 tablespoons water. Slowly whisk it into the broth and simmer 2 - 3 minutes, stirring often. Remove from heat. Add the sour cream to a medium bowl and stir in a few ladles of the hot broth to temper it then whisk the entire thing into the broth. Season to taste with salt and pepper. Make the Filling: Add the cream cheese to a large bowl with 1/2 cup of the warm broth. Stir until completely combined and smooth. Add the chicken, 1 cup of the cheese, the spinach, 1/2 teaspoon salt and 1/4 teaspoon black pepper. Mix until well combined. Assemble the Enchiladas: Preheat the oven to 400 degrees F. Butter a 9x13-inch casserole pan. Working one at a time add about 1/3 cup of the filling to one edge of the tortilla and spread it out like a log. Roll up the tortilla and place it in the pan seam side down. Repeat until all the filling is used, stacking them on top of each other if needed. Pour the sauce over the enchiladas. Sprinkle with the remaining cup of cheese. Bake 25 minutes. Let rest 5 minute before serving. Serve with sour cream plus any other toppings.

Baked Lemon Artichoke Chicken

{serves 4 – 6}

Bright and briny flavors are captured in these chicken breasts baked with artichoke hearts, capers, whole garlic cloves, Parmesan cheese and lemon slices. A one-pan meal easy enough for a busy weeknight.

1/4 cup extra-virgin olive oil, divided
1 + 1/2 - 2 pounds chicken cutlets
coarse salt and fresh black pepper
12 ounces artichoke hearts, jarred or frozen (thawed)
1/4 cup capers
8 cloves garlic, peeled
2 lemons, 1 of them zested and thinly sliced
2 - 3 tablespoons fresh grated Parmesan cheese, plus more for serving

1. Preheat the oven to 400 degrees F. Add 2 tablespoons of oil to a large roasting pan or baking sheet with sides - spread it out so the pan is greased well from edge to edge.

2. Cut the chicken cutlets in half and season them well with salt and pepper. Place them on the baking sheet, spreading them out so they're not touching.

3. In a medium bowl toss the artichoke hearts, capers, garlic and lemon slices with the remaining 2 tablespoons of oil, the lemon zest and a couple dashes of salt and pepper.

4. Arrange them all around the chicken in the pan, filling up the empty spaces and sprinkle the Parmesan all over them.

5. Bake until the chicken is cooked through anywhere from 25 - 45 minutes, depending on their size, internal temperature on a meat thermometer should reach 165 degrees F.

6. Cut the remaining lemon in half then into quarters. Serve with the lemon wedges for squeezing over top and Parmesan cheese.

Baked Broccoli Cheese Rice
{makes 8 servings as a side}

Rice and broccoli florets swimming in a creamy cheddar cheese sauce and baked until bubbly hot.

2 tablespoons butter, plus more for greasing pan
½ cup diced onion
2 cloves garlic, minced
2 tablespoons all-purpose flour
2 cups milk
1 tablespoon Dijon mustard
sea or kosher salt and fresh black pepper
2 + 1/2 cups shredded sharp cheddar cheese, divided
1/3 cup fresh grated Parmesan cheese
3 cups cooked brown or white rice
3 cups cooked broccoli florets

1. Grease a 9x9, 8x8 or 7x10-inch casserole dish. Preheat the oven to 400 degrees F.

2. In a large heavy-duty saucepan melt the butter over medium-low heat and add the onion and garlic. Cook 5 minutes, stirring often.

3. Sprinkle the flour over them and cook, stirring, 2 minutes.

4. Slowly whisk in the milk and turn the heat up slightly. Bring to a simmer and cook 2 – 3 minutes, stirring often.

5. Turn the heat down to medium-low and whisk in the mustard, ½ teaspoon salt and ¼ teaspoon black pepper. Add 2 cups of cheddar a little bit at a time and whisk until completely melted. Remove from heat.

6. Stir in the Parmesan. Stir in the rice and broccoli. Taste and season with more salt and pepper if needed.

7. Pour into the prepared pan and sprinkle the top with the remaining cheese.

8. Bake 25 – 30 minutes until bubbly and lightly golden on top. Let it set 5 – 10 minutes before serving.

Easy Cinnamon Roll Knots with Cream Cheese Dip

{makes 20 knots}

Puff pastry makes an easy shortcut for cinnamon roll knots stuffed with a buttery cinnamon filling on the inside and dusted with more cinnamon sugar to finish. Use the cream cheese icing as a dip or glaze.

Filling:
4 tablespoons butter, melted
1/4 cup granulated sugar
1 tablespoon ground cinnamon

Knots:
1 egg
1 tablespoon water
all-purpose flour, for dusting the work surface
1 9x9-inch frozen puff pastry sheet, thawed

Coating:
1/2 cup granulated sugar
2 tablespoons ground cinnamon

Glaze:
4 ounces cream cheese (regular or light)
a dash of vanilla extract
1/2 cup confectioners' sugar
3 - 4 tablespoons milk

Make the filling: In a small bowl mix together the butter, sugar and cinnamon until well combined. In a small bowl beat the egg and water together with a fork. Sprinkle a work surface with flour and unfold the pastry. Dust the top with flour and use a rolling pin to roll it out into a 10-inch square. Brush the bottom half of the pastry generously with beaten egg. Spoon all the filling over it and spread from edge to edge over the egg. Brush the top half with egg and fold it down over the filling. Roll the rolling pin lightly over it to help it stick together. Cut the pastry into 20 (1/2-inch-wide) strips with a paring knife or pizza cutter. Tie each strip into a "knot" and place on a parchment lined baking sheet. Place them in the freezer for at least 30 minutes to 1 hour. Preheat the oven to 400 degrees F. Place the knots on another parchment-lined baking sheet sprayed lightly with non-stick spray (don't use the frozen baking sheet to cook them) about an inch apart. Bake 18 - 20 minutes or until the pastries are golden brown - some of the cinnamon may leak out - that's normal. Meanwhile in a large mixing bowl whisk the sugar and cinnamon together for the coating. Use a spatula or big spoon to scoop up the knots a few at a time while they're hot and place them in the bowl. Toss gently in the cinnamon sugar. Remove to a wire rack or platter. Meanwhile melt the cream cheese in the microwave until it's soft and creamy about 20 - 30 seconds. Whisk in the confectioners' sugar and vanilla then enough milk to make a glaze. If it's too thin mix in a little more sugar – too thick stir in a little more milk. by mistake just mix in a little more sugar. Serve the knots warm or at room temperature with the dip. You can drizzle it over them instead if you like.

Cannoli Cream Stuffed Strawberries

Hollowed out strawberries filled with cannoli cream and garnished with chopped pistachios, chocolate chips and sprinkles. They're easy to make and are wonderful for potlucks, picnics, parties and showers too!

1 cup ricotta cheese (drain in a mesh strainer overnight or for a few hours ahead in fridge)
1 cup mascarpone cheese
1/8 teaspoon vanilla extract
1/2 cup confectioners' sugar, sifted
1/4 teaspoon cinnamon
the zest of 1 orange, just the top layer not the white pith
2 pounds of fresh strawberries
For garnish:
1/4 cup crushed pistachios
1/4 cup mini chocolate chips
rainbow sprinkles
melted chocolate, optional

1. In a medium mixing bowl on low speed beat the ricotta, mascarpone and vanilla until combined.

2. Beat in the confectioners' sugar, cinnamon and orange zest until creamy and well combined. Spoon into a pastry bag fitted with a large tip or into a large Ziploc bag. Refrigerate.

3. Wash the strawberries and pat dry with paper towels. Use the end of a potato peeler or a paring knife to remove the stem and cut a cone shape out of the center. Cut the tip so it stands flat. Line them up on a parchment lined baking sheet.

4. Pipe (or cut off one corner of your Ziploc bag) the cannoli cream into the strawberries and leave a nice dollop on top. If you fill them all and have some cream left go back over some of the bigger ones and put an extra dollop on them.

5. Garnish with pistachios, chocolate chips, sprinkles and drizzle with melted chocolate. Refrigerate.

6. These are best eaten within a few hours of making. You can prep everything a day ahead of time if you need them for a special occasion.

Southwestern Black Bean Mac & Cheese

Baked mac & cheese all dressed up with spicy pepper jack and sharp cheddar cheese, black beans and a crunchy tortilla chip topping.

12 ounces elbows
4 tablespoons butter, divided, plus more for greasing the pan
3 tablespoons all-purpose flour
2 cups milk
1 tablespoon Dijon mustard
2 cups shredded pepper jack cheese
2 cups shredded sharp cheddar cheese
sea or kosher salt and black pepper
14 ounce can black beans, drained, rinsed well & patted dry
Topping:
a couple handfuls of corn tortilla chips, crushed
a pat of butter, cut into small pieces

1. Cook the elbows to al dente in plenty of salted water according to package directions. Drain, add them back to the pan off the heat and toss with a tablespoon of butter to prevent sticking. Cover with a lid so they don't dry out.

2. Preheat the oven to 400 degrees F. Butter a 10-inch round or a 9x9-inch square casserole dish with high sides.

3. In a large, heavy-bottomed saucepan melt 3 tablespoons butter over medium-low heat. Stir in the flour and cook 3 minutes, stirring often. Slowly whisk in the milk and the mustard. Turn up the heat and bring to a simmer. Simmer, stirring often, 4 - 5 minutes.

4. Turn the heat down to low and add both cheeses holding back 1/2 cup for the top. Stir until completely melted and smooth. Remove from the heat and season with 1 teaspoon salt and 1/2 teaspoon black pepper.

5. Stir the black beans into the pasta. Pour the sauce over them and mix together gently with a wooden spoon.

6. Pour into the casserole dish. Sprinkle with the remaining cheese followed by the chips. Dot the top with the cut up butter.

7. Bake 25 minutes until bubbly all over and lightly golden on top. Let it sit 5 - 10 minutes before serving.

Oven-Fried Fish & Chips

{makes 4 servings}

Panko-coated cod baked until golden brown and flaky alongside Parmesan oven wedges and lemon-kissed tartar sauce.

1 + 1/2 pounds russet potatoes, scrubbed clean
1 - 2 teaspoons olive oil, plus more for greasing pans
coarse salt and fresh black pepper
1 cup Japanese panko crumbs
1/2 cup seasoned bread crumbs
1 pound cod fish
1/3 cup mayonnaise
2 - 3 tablespoons grated Parmesan cheese
1 heaping teaspoon chopped fresh parsley

Tartar sauce:
1/3 cup mayonnaise
2 - 3 tablespoons dill pickle relish or chopped dill pickles
the zest of one lemon, just the yellow layer not the white pith
malt vinegar, for serving

1. Preheat the oven to 400 degrees F. Grease a large cookie sheet. Cut the potatoes lengthwise into long 1-inch wide wedges. Place on cookie sheet and drizzle with oil. Toss with your hands then spread out on the baking sheet. Sprinkle with coarse salt and black pepper. Bake about 30 - 35 minutes until golden.

2. Meanwhile, set a cast iron skillet or small frying pan over medium heat and toast the panko crumbs, stirring often until lightly golden. Remove to a shallow bowl and allow to cool. Mix them with the seasoned bread crumbs.

3. Lightly grease a baking pan big enough to fit your fish in with oil. Use a pastry brush to coat the tops and sides of the fish with a thin layer of mayonnaise and season with salt and pepper. Coat the top and sides of the fish with the panko crumbs patting it on with your hands to help it adhere. Place the fish in the pan and sprinkle some of the remaining crumbs over top.

4. Bake 12 - 20 minutes depending on the size of your fish - check the middle - the fish should be white and not translucent in the center. Meanwhile, make the tartar sauce by mixing the mayonnaise, dill pickles and lemon zest together in a small bowl.

5. When the potatoes are cooked toss with the Parmesan and parsley. Serve with tartar sauce and malt vinegar for the fries, if desired.

Slice & Bake Pizza Roll-ups

{makes 12}

All the flavors of pizza surrounded by flaky, melt-in-your-mouth puff pastry! They're the perfect make ahead appetizers because you can assemble them ahead of time, freeze and pop them out as needed.

1 (9x9) puff pastry sheet, thawed
1/3 cup pizza sauce
1/4 teaspoon dried oregano or Italian seasoning
sea or kosher salt and fresh black pepper
1 + 1/3 cups shredded mozzarella cheese
1/4 cup diced pepperoni
1 tablespoon grated Parmesan cheese
salt and fresh ground black pepper
chopped parsley or basil, for garnish, optional

1. On a lightly floured surface unfold the puff pastry. Spread the sauce from edge to edge leaving about a 1-inch border on one of the longest sides.

2. Sprinkle the oregano over the sauce, crushing it between your fingertips. Season lightly with salt and pepper.

3. Sprinkle the mozzarella, pepperoni and Parmesan evenly from edge to edge.

4. Roll the pastry up toward the 1-inch border keeping the roll as tight as you can. Wrap in plastic wrap. To maintain the round shape you can stick it inside a cardboard paper towel roll that has been cut lengthwise.

5. Stick it in the freezer for about an hour (or longer if you want to make them ahead of time for a party or special occasion).

6. Preheat oven to 400 degrees F. Line a baking sheet with parchment paper or grease it well.

7. If the pizza roll has been frozen for longer than an hour then you should let it sit out on the counter 15 - 20 minutes before slicing.

8. Use a sharp paring knife to cut the roll into 3/4-inch thick slices. Lay them 1 - 2 inches apart on the cookie sheet.

9. Bake 18 - 20 minutes until puffy and golden brown. Let cool on the baking sheet 5 minutes before serving. Sprinkle with fresh chopped parsley or basil.

Creamy Chicken Enchilada Soup
{makes 6 servings}

Sour cream chicken enchiladas brought to life in a delicious, semi-spicy soup!

3 tablespoons olive oil, divided
1 pound boneless chicken breasts, cut into bite-sized pieces
sea or kosher salt and fresh black pepper
1 large yellow onion, diced
1 large green or red bell pepper, diced
3 cloves garlic, minced
2 teaspoons chili powder
1/2 teaspoon ground cumin
1/2 teaspoon dried oregano, crushed between fingertips
1 can (11 ounce) Ro-tel diced tomatoes & green chiles
4 cups low-sodium chicken broth
2 cups corn
2 tablespoons corn starch
1 cup sour cream, plus more for serving
1 + 1/2 cups shredded sharp cheddar or Monterey jack cheese, plus more for serving
tortilla chips, for serving

1. In a Dutch oven or large soup pot heat 1 tablespoon oil over medium heat. Add the chicken and season well with salt and pepper. Cook 2 – 3 minutes per side, turning to sear on all sides. Remove to a small bowl and set aside.

2. Add the remaining 2 tablespoons oil to the pan with the onions, peppers and garlic. Season with salt and pepper. Cook until softened, stirring often, about 10 minutes. Add the chicken back to the pan with the chili powder, cumin and oregano. Stir to coat everything with the spices and cook 2 minutes, stirring often. Stir in the Ro-tel, broth, corn, ½ teaspoon salt and ¼ teaspoon black pepper. Bring up to a simmer and cook, stirring often 25 minutes.

3. In a small bowl whisk the cornstarch with ¼ cup water. Slowly whisk it into the soup and let it cook 5 minutes. In the same bowl mix the sour cream with a ladle or two of soup to temper it then repeat. Stir it into the soup. Stir in the cheese. Bring back to a simmer and stir until the cheese is melted. Remove from heat.

4. Season to taste with more salt and pepper if needed. Serve with a garnish of cheese and a dollop of sour cream plus chips for dipping and scooping.

www.ingramcontent.com/pod-product-compliance
Lightning Source LLC
Chambersburg PA
CBHW081354080526
44588CB00016B/2496